I0191174

Good Stress - Bad Stress

How to thrive in today's challenging environments!

Troy Rath

Copyright © 2015 Troy Rath

All rights reserved.

ISBN:13- **978-0-9967439-1-4**
ISBN-099674391x

To my wife, my friend, my true companion.

I Love you!

CONTENTS

ACKNOWLEDGMENTS

I would like to thank Dr. Angela Priester for her help and guidance on this project. I would also like to thank Nicole Lynch and Terri Rath for their editing expertise.

CHAPTER 1

AN OVERVIEW OF STRESS

How can we grow and thrive in a fast paced stressful environment?

Stress is a common condition that all of us encounter as we live our daily lives. It cannot, and as we will learn, should not be avoided. It is stress that enables us to grow and thrive and take on life's demands.

Stress is short for distress. It is derived from a Latin word meaning "to rend or pull apart."

Dr. Walter Cannon in his work, "The Wisdom of the Body" described stress as, "external influences that disrupt homeostasis."

Homeostasis:
Our body's biochemical ability to react and adapt to our environment in order to maintain internal conditions.

Examples of Homeostatic Regulation:

Our bodies will try to maintain an internal temperature of 98.6° F or 37° C. If we are exposed to conditions that cause this temperature to rise, our bodies start to perspire. To ensure proper cellular metabolism the body regulates blood sugar through the release of insulin. If an individual engages in strength exercise, muscular growth will result.

The body reacts and adapts to its conditions.

Stress is typically thought of today as conditions that evoke mental or emotional tension.

Stress has been made the villain.

It has been blamed for:
- Accelerated aging
- Hypertension
- Cardiovascular disease
- Type II diabetes
- Arthritis
- High cholesterol
- Stroke

Stress is like the Dr. Jekyll and Mr. Hyde story. Much of the time it is beneficial and at other times it is monstrous and even dangerous to our health. Short periods of physical, mental and emotional challenges, when followed by recovery, will lead to growth and adaptation. Chronic stress is unrelenting and destructive.

Is stress truly the villain we have made it out to be?

Our bodies are continually adapting to our environmental conditions. As we mature, we take on new responsibilities, such as school, work, family, or even retirement. Stressful conditions such as a final exam or a fast approaching deadline at work can be very stressful. Yet, it is these conditions that allow us to push ourselves to new limits and grow our abilities.

Stress becomes the catalyst that initiates adaptation in the form of growth, thus preparing to handle even more the next time we are stressed. However, if we want to excel in any category of life it requires a pattern of stress and recovery.

The correct balance between exertion and recovery results in growth.

Too much or too
little exertion
results in
atrophy.

Too much or too
little recovery
results in
atrophy.

How will you take on life's challenges and grow without being overly stressed? How will you learn to be able to handle more as you gain experience? If we want to excel in any category of life it requires a pattern of stress and recovery.

To apply your energy effectively and efficiently you need to recover effectively and efficiently. It is through this pattern of intense effort and recovery that you will increase your potential and be able to excel. To effectively apply your energy, connect to what you are trying to accomplish. Be eager to get up every day to pursue your goals. Be eager to get home every evening to reenergize. Immerse yourself in your personal vision and you will fundamentally shift how you live your life.

The Secret Formula for Success

 **+**  **=**

| **Work** | **Recovery** | **Success** |

Balancing exertion and recovery today will allow you to do more tomorrow.

CHAPTER 2

THE FIGHT-OR-FLIGHT RESPONSE
(the acute stress response)

The body's reaction to what it perceives as a threat or challenge.

The body's autonomic nervous system is comprised of the **sympathetic** and **parasympathetic** nervous systems.

The **Sympathetic** nervous system responds to a threat or challenge by preparing for action (fight-or-flight).

The **Parasympathetic** nervous system returns the body to a relaxed state after the threat has passed (rest and digest).

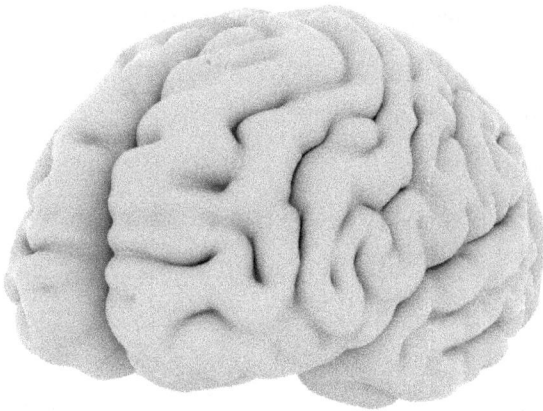

When a threat is perceived by the brain and the sympathetic nervous system activates, a sequence of events takes place resulting in the body being prepared for action.

When the fight-or-flight reaction occurs, the pituitary gland releases adrenocorticotropic hormone (ACTH). This triggers the adrenal glands to release the neural transmitter epinephrine that results in the release of cortisol.

Changes from the release of cortisol include:
- Increased blood pressure, heart rate, respiration and blood glucose for extra energy
- Increased blood flow to muscles providing additional speed and strength.
- Increased blood clotting in the event of an injury
- Dilated pupils providing increased vision clarity
- Increased perspiration to prevent over-heating
- Decreased emphasis on hearing and "tunnel vision" focusing attention on the threat
- Increase of activity within the cerebellum that provides immediate access to physical skills

The hormone Oxytocin is also released at this time. Oxytocin is the feel good chemical that encourages socialization, bonding and action. It will direct your energy toward the challenge you are facing, it will encourage you to seek help and it provides the endurance to carry you through.

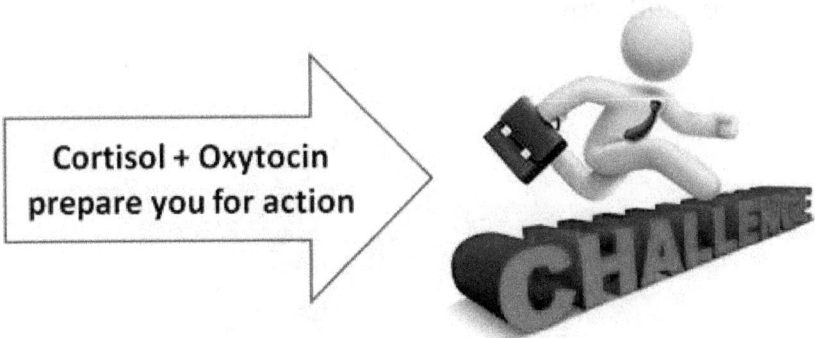

This is your body's natural reaction to life's challenges.

Rest and Digest
Parasympathetic Nervous System

When the perceived threat is gone, the body will return to its normal state through the release of the neurotransmitter acetylcholine. The high alert condition caused by cortisol will be turned off, allowing the body to recover and grow.

CHAPTER 3

CHRONIC STRESS

What happens when the state of stress continues without recovery?

Without relief, the body keeps redirecting energy away from functions such as digestion, the immune system and reproduction and directs it to respiration, circulation and muscular function.

Since the perceived threat continues, the adrenal release of cortisol continues and the body does not recover (rest and digest.)

Stress is not harmful over a short period of time. However, prolonged over a period of weeks, months or years it can become very harmful. Fight-or-flight may prepare you for action but it is not the ideal state for daily life.

Chronic over-secretion of stress hormones adversely affects brain function, especially memory. The research of Stanford University professor Dr. Robert M. Sapolsky has demonstrated that sustained high levels of cortisol can damage the hippocampus due to the prolonged redirection of blood glucose. When the hippocampus is continually exposed to too much cortisol, the brain's ability to produce new memories or access existing memories is inhibited.

Ohio State University's Dr. Janice Kiecolt-Glaser's has documented the detrimental effects of chronic stress. She links stress to accelerated aging, several types of cancer, cardiovascular disease, type II diabetes, arthritis, high cholesterol, heart disease and stroke. Chronic stress also promotes behaviors such as overeating, smoking, and substance abuse.

It has been theorized that up to 90% of all doctor's visits can be attributed to directly or indirectly to stress. Stress, resulting in hypertension, suppresses the body's immune system and reduces your ability to sleep, which, in turn, makes you vulnerable to all manner of illness. This includes high blood pressure, heart disease, stroke, arteriosclerosis and kidney failure.

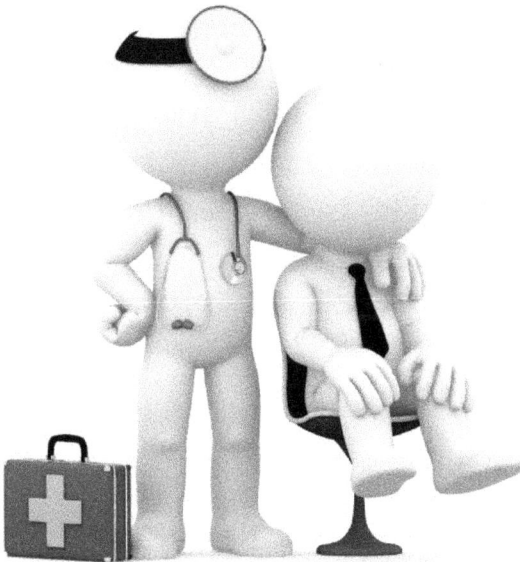

The potential causes of stress are numerous and highly individualized. What causes stress depends in part on your perception of the circumstances. Something that is stressful to you may not faze someone else. The situations and pressures that cause stress are known as *stressors*. We usually think of stressors as being negative, such as an exhausting work schedule. However, anything that puts high demands on you can be stressful. This includes positive events such as getting married, buying a house, going off to college, or starting a new job.

The three types of stressors are:

1. **Incidental** – This occurs somewhat randomly, such as someone is rude to you and you become angry. This is typically short in duration.
2. **Fatigue** – This can be physical and mental in nature. For example, when someone keeps pushing and pushing themselves due to an overly busy schedule without sufficient recovery.
3. **Anticipatory** – This is stress resulting from the anticipation of an event or its consequences. This can continue for weeks or months.

Too much stress is often the result of the compounding and continuation of multiple stressors. It can be like wading into the ocean. If you wade out into water up to your knees and a small wave comes along, it will push you a little but it won't be overwhelming. But what if you waded out into water up to your neck? Then even smallest waves would be over your head.

If you are relatively stress free, issues that arise are typically easy to handle. But, if you carry stress with you so you feel up to your neck, then even the smallest of issues can make you feel like you are drowning, and your ability to address these or any other challenges in life is greatly diminished.

It is important to recognize when you are chronically in a highly stressed condition.

Almost any emotional state over time can feel normal. People learn to cope with their conditions and become numb to the discomfort. It becomes their new normal. They can even miss it when it is not there, but that doesn't mean it is not unhealthy.

Signs that you may be under too much stress:
- You continually feel irritated.
- You respond to even minor irritants with anger.
- You have difficulty controlling your emotions.
- You are unable to relax and have fun.
- You find yourself feeling discouraged and wanting to quit.
- You are chronically tired.
- You resort to artificial means of relaxing such as drinking alcohol.
- You spend a large amount of time overly concerned with money, health, the future…

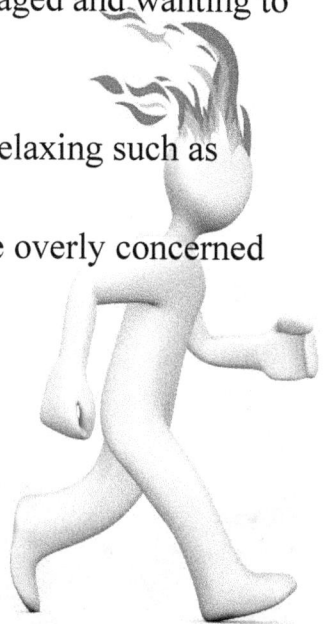

CHAPTER 4

STOPPING CHRONIC STRESS

If the estimates of the negative impacts that chronic stress has had our society are even close to being correct, then this is our number one health risk. It is within one's control to address it.

It is available to be happier, healthier and more productive. But, if we run our daily lives like a marathon, we will soon be out of energy and vulnerable to the effects of chronic stress. We may keep going but we will not be functioning at the level we could be. We will not perform optimally at work or at home and we could be in jeopardy of losing our health and happiness.

Remember, you do not want to eliminate stress from your life. You do want to find a balance of stress and recovery to facilitate personal growth.

The challenge we face living in today's fast paced world is to not remain chronically in a state of stress. We must interweave periods which facilitate recovery into our lives. Doing so will go a long way to curtailing chronic stress.

The three primary ways of stemming the tide of chronic stress in your life are:

☑ Break stress' continuity

☑ Change your reaction

☑ Remove the cause

Break Stress' Continuity
Living Life in Intervals

We cannot maintain a happy, healthy and productive lifestyle in the midst of continuous stress. It will quickly catch up with us. In this state it is difficult to experience the richness and joys of life. Mental, physical and emotional fatigue will dominate. Your ability to accomplish intended tasks will be limited, and therefore, your results will be limited. People are not designed to live life as a continuous exertion. Rather, we are designed to excel in a series of sprints mixed with periods of refreshment. When we focus and fully exert ourselves and then we replenish the energy that was expended so we can return to a period of focused exertion.

If you are moving continuously from one activity to another and another, while not recovering, fatigue will build, emotions may run high and there will be minimal recovery. For many people this is life: going to work, coming home, taking care of the kids, the house… and no time for themselves.

Tips for Living Life in Intervals

Daily:
- Take breaks every 60 – 90 minutes
- Get up and walk around
- Drink water/snack
- Stretch
- Change activities if possible
- Keep a consistent schedule
- Get enough sleep
- Eat well
- Exercise

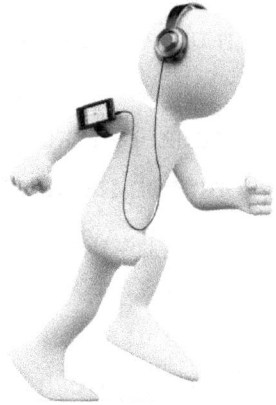

Weekly:
- Take at least one day off per week

Yearly:
- Vacation

Recovery time is not wasting time. Rather it is an essential part of a high performance lifestyle. It will help ensure that the time you spend on task can have the highest quality and quantity of energy possible associated with it

Breaking Stress' Continuity - A Strategic Diet

It requires energy for the body to function. We obtain our energy through the food we consume. Ensure that the food you eat is meeting the body's needs. A healthy diet means a healthier, more energetic and more successful you.

What should you eat?

Eat food with high nutritional density. These are typically unprocessed foods as close to how nature provided them as possible. Most of your diet should be comprised of these types of foods. Highly processed foods, such as a hamburger, fries and cola should comprise the minority of what you consume.

When and how much should you eat?

There is more to a diet than what you eat. When, you eat and how much you eat is also important. Strategic caloric placement provides a consistent supply of blood glucose. Consistent blood glucose provides consistent energy and facilitates effective recovery. Eating often is essential for consistent blood glucose, but this does not mean eating more. It means eating smaller meals and healthy snacks distributed throughout the day.

Do you ever skip breakfast? If you do, your body will have to find energy from somewhere. By lunch time you will be starving. These circumstances will likely result in cravings for a large, fatty, high-calorie meal. If you eat that meal another issue emerges, namely, what to do with all those calories. The body reacts and adapts to its conditions. A dietary pattern that continually places the body in a low blood glucose condition by having only two or three large meals with several hours in between is teaching your body that food is scarce and you need to store some reserves.

This pattern of low blood glucose followed by a sudden glut of calories can also lower your metabolism. After restoring the blood glucose, your body will happily place the excess into storage as fat. Fat cells are the only cells of the body that have the capacity to absorbing the extra calories. Meanwhile, your body diverts energy to the task of digestion and fat storage, resulting in feeling lethargic.

Blood glucose is the fuel for the cells in your body. If you don't eat frequently enough and use up your glycogen stores, your body must find glucose from somewhere. There are two choices, body fat or lean body tissue. There is more energy in fat than lean tissue, but if the body has been placed into a condition that indicates that food is scarce, then for the short term, lean tissue will be used and the fat stores will be saved in case the "emergency" continues. So, if you are consistently placing yourself in a low blood glucose condition, your body will burn lean body tissues, save the fat and then send messages to the brain urging you to eat sugary, fatty foods. This solves both of the perceived issues by providing the blood with more glucose and storing additional energy in case the condition continues.

By employing a dietary strategy that maintains your blood glucose level through more frequent, smaller meals, your body will raise its metabolism and freely apply your energy to whatever task is at hand, thereby enabling brain and other bodily functions to help you address any stressful conditions in life. You will be able to apply more energy to what you are doing without the highs and lows associated with a poor diet.

Breaking Stress' Continuity - Exercise

Vigorous exercise causes the body to release hormones called endorphins. Produced by the central nervous system and the pituitary gland, the primary purpose of endorphins is to inhibit the sensation of pain by acting as a natural analgesic, thus producing a sensation of euphoria.

Endorphins bind to the same neural receptors as medicines such as morphine. The difference is that endorphins' activation of these receptors does not lead to addiction.

Distance athletes often have a euphoric feeling or "runner's high." This is due to the prolonged production of endorphins during exercise.

Endorphin release during regular exercise has been proven to:
- Reduce stress and anxiety
- Reduce the feelings of depression
- Boost self-esteem
- Improve sleep

Breaking Stress' Continuity
Immediate Relief from High Stress

If you can interrupt stress you can recover and implement changes for a long-term solution.

Take long, slow deep breaths
Breathing is the one part of the fight or flight response that is controllable by your conscious mind. When you are highly stressed, you can breathe slowly and deeply to send signals that the emergency has passed. This will help shut off sympathetic nervous system and turn on the parasympathetic system so you can recover.

Stress reduction exercise (used to stop extreme stress)
As the human brain becomes highly stressed, it reduces the communication between the two hemispheres of the cerebral cortex. These stressful thoughts result in an unbroken pattern of thoughts recurring in the right side of the brain. But, you can use how the brain works to interrupt this pattern and thereby disrupt this condition.

Breaking Stress' Continuity
Stress Reduction Exercise

The techniques below will provide an immediate break to the pattern of stress. Do this whenever you feel overly stressed or panicky.

Focusing Breath:
- 5 -7 second inhale, hold for 2 seconds, 5 – 7 second exhale
  - Count the seconds. Don't cut it short.
  - Breathe deeply from your diaphragm.

Play Catch with Yourself:
- Take a small ball, bean bag or even a crumpled sheet of paper. Separate your hands by at least 3 feet. Toss the ball back and forth between your hands for 30 – 60 seconds.

Sensory Input:
- Eat something that tastes pleasurable. Chocolate works well.

Cleansing Breath:
- 5 -7 second inhale, hold for 2 seconds, 5 – 7 second exhale
  - Breathe deeply from your diaphragm.

This may seem overly simple, but it really works!

Change Your Reaction

Dr Albert Ellis developed Rational Emotive Behavior Therapy (REBT). REBT is based upon the principle that people are not disturbed by events but rather by their view of events. The sequence shown below is the basic flow of an activating event stimulating a belief which results in an emotional response.

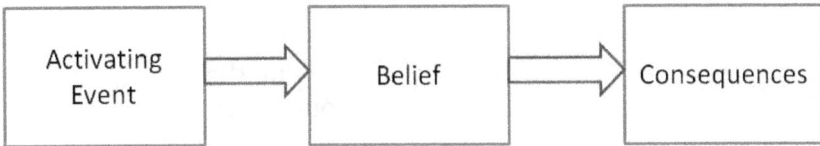

Activating Event	→	Belief	→	Consequences
This is an event that you experience.		Your beliefs (view) regarding yourself in these conditions.		Your emotional response based on your beliefs.

This pattern works fine unless an individual holds irrational beliefs concerning themselves regarding the activating event. Then the consequence or result will come from that irrational view.

Change Your Reaction

Your belief which initiates your reaction (consequences) is a subjective interpretation of what happened (activating event). This typically occurs automatically.

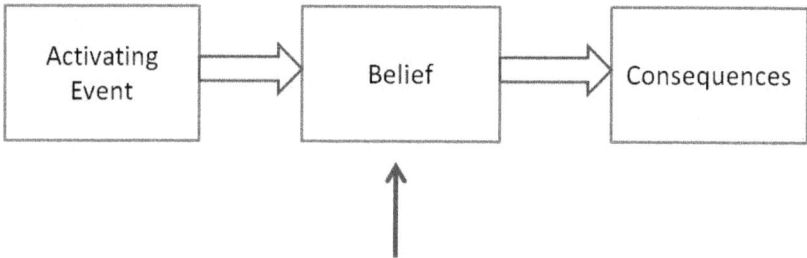

| Activating Event | → | Belief | → | Consequences |

↑

You can intervene and change the outcome by disputing your belief.

"Between stimulus and response there is a space. In that space is our power to choose our response. In our response lies our growth and our freedom."
– Victor Frankl

| Activating Event | → | Belief | → | Consequences |

↑

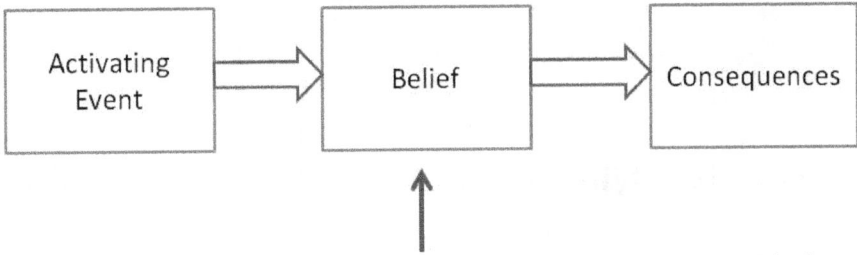

Change your reaction – Dispute your belief

A. **Activating event**: This is an event that you experience.
B. **Beliefs:** Your beliefs regarding yourself under these conditions.
C. **Consequence:** You have an emotional response based on your beliefs.

What if your belief is irrational? Then the consequence or result will most likely be irrational.

To address an irrational belief one can:
D. **Dispute:** Counteract the irrational belief with a rational one.
E. New **Emotion:** When you have successfully disputed the irrational belief, then new beliefs and subsequent emotions can emerge.

Cognitive Behavior Stress Reduction Exercise

To assist you with disputing an irrational belief there is a four part exercise.

1. Identify the activating event.
   - Identify the cause of the stress.

2. Identify your beliefs concerning the event.
   - Often, determining how you feel can help identify the belief behind it.

3. List the potential consequences or outcomes due to the activating event.
   - Most continuing stress is caused by the anticipation of future events. By listing the potential outcomes it typically becomes clear that it things aren't as bad as they first appeared.

4. Make a list of things to dispute the irrational belief
   - These are rational ways of reacting to the activating event.

Cognitive Behavior Stress Reduction Exercise Example

1. **Activating Event**
   - You get an email asking you to take on an additional project at work.

2. **Beliefs**
   - I do not have the time to do my current work.
   - How will I be able to add this to my schedule?
   - Don't they realize I am already overloaded?
   - Things are so busy at home.

3. **Consequences**
   - You become more stressed and all of your activities suffer.
   - Negative emotions (fear, anxiety…)
   - Complain to coworkers, family…

4. **Dispute**
   - It is only for a short time. I can do this.
   - I can ask for help on my other work.
   - I should discuss with my supervisor this to find the best balance.
   - This shows my work is valued.

When you effectively dispute your belief, it can result in a new belief and therefore a new outcome.

Change Your Reaction
After Your Interpretation of the Event

Your view of the activating event has now determined a resulting behavior.

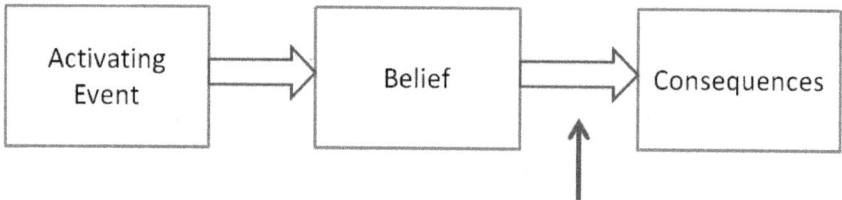

```
┌──────────────┐        ┌──────────────┐        ┌──────────────┐
│  Activating  │ ═══▶   │    Belief    │ ═══▶   │ Consequences │
│    Event     │        │              │        │              │
└──────────────┘        └──────────────┘        └──────────────┘
                                ▲
                                │
```

Disputing at this point can be a battle because you are up against an emotionally charged intention.
An irrational response will often overestimate the severity of the event.

Dispute the irrational with the rational.

Change Your Reaction
Addressing Irrational Overreactions

If your reaction to the activating event is irrational, typically your mind has over-estimated the likelihood, severity or duration of the event by considering worst case scenarios.

Dispute the irrational through rational arguments.
* What is the probability it will actually occur?
* What is the most likely outcome?
* Have I overreacted before for no reason?
* What are the best and worst case scenarios?

Remove the Cause

We have the ability to choose. We can choose our environment and those who we associate with. If there is something around that affects you negatively, you can make changes to reduce or eliminate its influence. Thoughts are real, with real effects.

Why would someone voluntarily expose themselves to something that is detrimental? It could be music that expresses anger at the world, A TV show that embraces envy, jealously and dishonesty or video games where the object is to kill everything. The information is processed and reacted to by the mind. Let's say you are going to watch a movie that is very violent and frightening. Your conscious mind may say, "I know that is not real. It's OK." But if it has entered your mind, it has had an effect, it has caused anxiety and the effects have been felt. How could that effect be positive?

Our state of mind is the result of a chemical balance controlled by the limbic system in our brain. It reacts to all the thoughts running through the brain and releases a chemical mixture that it has been trained to release under similar circumstances. It does not wonder why and it doesn't distinguish between reality and fiction. If you watch a stressful movie it responds as if you are actually experiencing it. No one is immune. To be "immune," would be contrary to how we function as humans. Let's not give ourselves any more of an uphill battle than we already have.

Control what information you voluntarily expose your mind to. Control who you are with and what you do. Endeavor to have your environment positively contribute to your efforts. This will go a long way to help you reduce stress in your life.

Conclusion

Managing stress is about taking charge of your thoughts, your emotions, your schedule, your environment, and the way you deal with challenges. It is about adequate recovery to ensure you are ready to address whatever your future holds.

Remember, you do not want to eliminate stress from your life. Rather, you should find a balance between stress and recovery to facilitate personal growth.

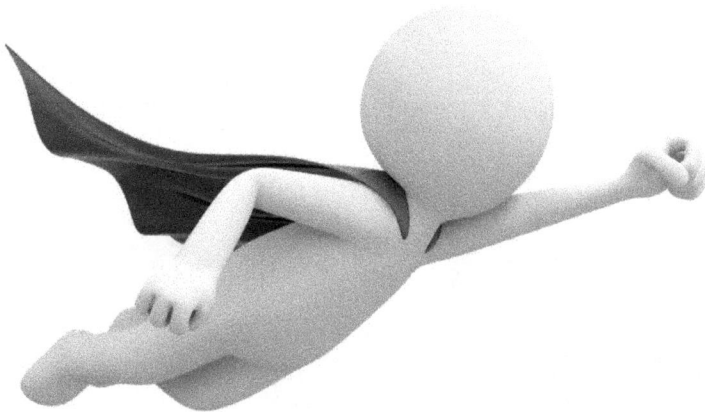

Notes

P. 3. Cannon, Walter. The Wisdom of the Body. New York, NY: Norton & Company, 1939. Print.

P 8. Christyn L. Dolbier, ShannaE. Smith, Mary A. Stienhardt. Stress-Related Growth: Correlates and Change Following a Residence Intervention. Web.
http://www.edb.utexas.edu/steinhardt/Files/Dolbier.Smith.Steinhardt.J CC(112208).pdf

P. 15. Mark Schwartz. "Robert Sapolsky discusses physiological effects of stress." Stanford University. March 7, 2007. Web.
http://news.stanford.edu/news/2007/march7/sapolskysr-030707.html

P. 16. "Janice Kiecolt-Glaser" Ohio State University. Web.
http://faculty.psy.ohio-state.edu/1/kiecolt-glaser/

P. 17. Marcelina Hardy. "Five Types of stressors." Love to Know. Web.
http://www.webmd.com/depression/guide/exercise-depression

P. 17. "Different Kinds of Stress." DIY Stress Relief. June 30, 2015. Web.
http://www.diy-stress-relief.com/kinds-of-stress.html

P. 23 – 26. Jim Loehr, Tony Schwartz. The Power of Full Engagement. Ney York, NY: The Free Press, 2003. Print.

P. 27. "Exercise and Depression." WebMD. Web.
http://www.webmd.com/depression/guide/exercise-depression

P. 28. "Corpus Callosum Function." Steady Health. Web.
http://ic.steadyhealth.com/corpus_callosum_function.html

P. 28. Eric Mooshagian. "Anatomy of the Corpus Callosum Reveals Its Function." The Journal of Neuroscience. February 13. 2008. Web.
http://www.jneurosci.org/content/28/7/1535.full

P. 30. William Ross. "What is REBT." REBT Network. Web.
http://www.rebtnetwork.org/whatis.html

P. 28, 30-32, 35. Albert Ellis. "REBT." REBT. Web.
http://www.rebt.ws/REBT%20explained.htm

P. 28, 30 - 36. Jason Satterfield. "Coping with Stress: Cognitive-Behavioral Stress Reaction." University of California Television. August 31, 2012. Web. http://www.youtube.com/watch?v=0BbHW3H_xmo

Providing innovative ideas for a modern world.

Troy Rath

www.ingramcontent.com/pod-product-compliance
Lightning Source LLC
Chambersburg PA
CBHW060042040426
42331CB00032B/2182